W9-BXE-808

UGLY ANIMALS

By Gilda & Melvin Berger

SCHOLASTIC INC.

NEW YORK   TORONTO   LONDON   AUCKLAND

SYDNEY   MEXICO CITY   NEW DELHI   HONG KONG

SCHOLASTIC READER

LEVEL **3**

700-1500 WORDS

Photo credits:
Front Cover © Rob Cousins/Alamy; Back cover © Paul A. Souders/Corbis; Page 3 (top left) © imagebroker/
Alamy, (top right) © Paul A. Souders/Corbis, (bottom left) © dbimages/Alamy, (bottom right) © National
Geographic Image Collection/Alamy; Pages 4-5 © Juniors Bildarchiv/Alamy; Page 6 © John Sutcliffe/Alamy;
Pages 8-9 © Frans Lanting/Corbis; Page 10 © Luis Louro/Shutterstock; Page 13 © Chris Hellier/Alamy;
Pages 14-15 © Rod Planck/Photo Researchers, Inc.; Page 16 © John Cancalosi/Alamy; Page 17 © Milaniluc/
iStockphoto; Page 19 © Rob Cousins/Alamy; Page 20 © SeaPics; Pages 22-23 © SeaPics; Page 25 © John
Carnemolla/Australian Picture Library/Corbis; Page 26 © WILDLIFE GmbH/Alamy; Pages 28-29 © ANT Photo
Library/Photo Researchers, Inc.; Pages 30-31 © Blue Gum Pictures/Alamy

ISBN 978-0-545-34663-4

10 9 8 7 6 5 4   12 13 14 15 16/0

Printed in the U.S.A.   40
First printing, September 2011

What makes an animal **"UGLY?"**
Often, it is some feature that makes
one animal different from others.

FUNNY HAIR

SHARP HORNS

A HUGE NOSE

A BLUE TONGUE

Each of these features is extremely unusual.
They may strike you as strange. But there's a
reason for every feature. It helps the animal
survive in its *environment*. Now, let's meet
some of the world's ugliest animals!

The **KOMONDOR DOG** has long, thick ropes of white hair. The hair hangs down like strings on a mop. It gets longer as the dog grows older. Male komondors actually have the heaviest fur of all dogs!

Why do komondor dogs have such thick hair? These dogs once were used to herd sheep. The dogs' heavy fur kept them safe from attack by wolves or bears. Today, komondors make good pets. They still have very thick coats, but they can run surprisingly fast.

The BABIRUSA is a wild pig. Males have four huge tusks on their head. Two tusks grow from its bottom jaw and two from its top jaw. Its diet is mainly made up of fruit, seeds, berries, and insects. It also digs in the ground with its hooves to find the roots and shoots of young plants.

The male barbirusa uses its tusks to protect its eyes when it fights with other males. When two males fight, they stand on their hind legs and butt each other.

Almost everyone agrees that the **NAKED MOLE RAT** has many ugly features. It only has a few hairs on its body and four long teeth on the outside of its mouth. Its eyes and ears are tiny. And its legs and tail are very short.

But thanks to its unusual looks, the naked mole rat gets along just fine. It lives in underground tunnels that it digs with its huge front teeth. Its teeth are in front of its lips so it doesn't get dirt in its mouth. Its smooth body also lets the naked mole rat crawl easily through these tunnels. There it is safe from eagles and other enemies.

The face of the UAKARI MONKEY is as red as a tomato! No one knows exactly why. People used to think uakaris had bright red faces because they spent too much time in the sun. They noticed that the red color faded when the monkeys were kept out of the sunlight.

In the Amazon rain forest where they live, uakari monkeys are few and far apart. Some think their bright red faces help them find one another among the thick trees. Others say it is more likely that their red faces are a sign of good health.

Noses come in all sizes. But the male
PROBOSCIS MONKEY has the
biggest nose of all! Some say it looks
like a banana. Why such a big, ugly nose?
Perhaps it's because female *proboscis*
monkeys seem to prefer males with
large noses.

The male proboscis monkey honks loudly
to keep in touch with other monkeys. The
nose's large size makes the sound deeper
to warn others of danger and to keep the
group together. With each "honk" its nose
pops straight out.

The nose of the **STAR-NOSED MOLE** is bizarre. It looks like a star! The points of the star are like tiny fingers that the animal uses to touch and feel. This mole uses its star-shaped nose to find food at the bottom of ponds and streams. It waves the "fingers" in the water to catch worms, bugs, and shellfish. No other animal has a better sense of touch!

The star-nosed mole is nearly blind. But it is a good swimmer and hunts for its food in water day and night—even in winter. This animal has been seen digging tunnels in the snow and swimming in ice-covered streams.

The **SHOVEL-NOSED FROG** takes its name from its sharp, pointy nose. Why does this frog need a "shovel" at the tip of its _snout_? It uses it to make tunnels in the mud as it looks for food to eat. The hard tip at the end is great for pushing away soil and digging out earthworms. In the rainy wet season, this frog shovels its way out of its _burrow_ to hunt after dark. In the dry season, the snout helps the frog move quickly through loose soil.

The **SHOEBILL BIRD** has a huge bill that looks like a clog, or wooden shoe. You may think the bill looks clumsy and ugly. But the shoebill bird really needs it. A strong bill helps the bird catch and hold the slippery fish, turtles, and young crocodiles that it feeds on. To warn of danger, the bird loudly claps the two parts of its bill together. When not in use, it rests the heavy bill on its neck!

The **AYE-AYE** is so-o-o ugly. It has large, staring eyes, and ears that look much too big for its body. And its fingers are as thin as wires.

Huge eyes and skinny fingers are a huge help for *nocturnal* animals. The aye-aye uses its large eyes and ears to help it hunt in the forest at night. It taps on trees with its long fingers until it finds a bug. Then it makes a hole in the wood and pulls out its dinner.

ANGLERFISH are strange and scary.
A long spine sticks up above the fish's eyes.
It has a fleshy growth at the end that looks
like a light at the tip of a tiny fishing pole.
The anglerfish uses it to hunt for food.

The anglerfish wiggles the growth.
Predators think it is something to eat.
This "bait" lures them closer and closer.
Then SNAP! The anglerfish grabs the
prey with its needle-sharp teeth—and
swallows the fish whole.

Can you imagine a fish with lipstick? Well, meet the **RED-LIPPED BATFISH**! It has thick lips that are bright red and most unusual in a fish. This animal spends most of its time on the ocean floor looking for food. Its heavy lips are excellent for scooping up shrimp, crabs, small fish, and worms.

Red lips are not the only odd feature of this fish. The red-lipped batfish is a fish that can barely swim! Instead, it uses its big fins like feet and walks on the sandy bottom of the sea!

The **BLUE-TONGUED SKINK** is a large lizard with a big head and long body. It lives mostly in open country, among grasses and leaves. Insects, flowers, and berries are its favorite foods.

But some animals are so ugly that they can scare away their enemies. The blue-tongued skink is such a creature. It cannot move very fast. When in danger, it sticks a shocking blue tongue out of its bright pink mouth. That is usually enough to stop a predator in its tracks.

The male **HOODED SEAL** has a droopy muzzle, or nose, with a flap. It hangs down like a hood over its nose. The flap grows bigger as the seal grows older.

When the seal gets frightened, it blows up the flap. Then the nose looks like a big red balloon! Enemies find the seal so scary that they run away.

One look at a **PIG-NOSED TURTLE** and you know where it got its name. Its snout is shaped like that of a tiny pig with two nostrils! This strange-looking turtle makes its home in freshwater rivers, lakes, and streams.

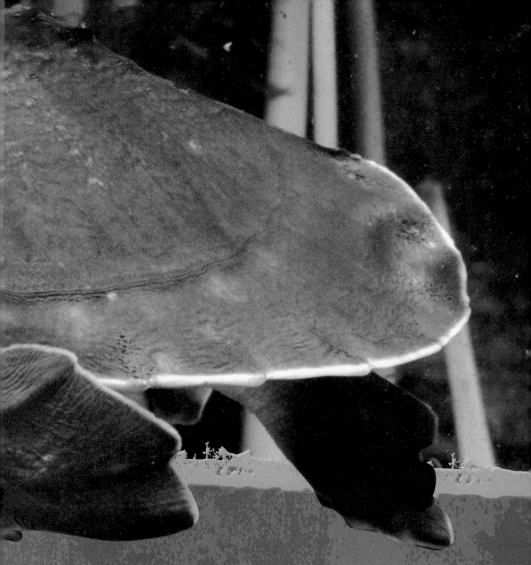

Pig-nosed turtles are different from all other freshwater turtles. Instead of front legs, they have two broad flippers or paddles. Also, their back legs have webbing between the toes. It's not surprising that pig-nosed turtles are good, fast swimmers.

The **THORNY DEVIL** is a lizard that lives in the desert. Its body is the color of sand, which lets the lizard blend in with its surroundings.

But the lizard also has another helpful, but ugly, feature. Many hard, sharp thorns cover its body and hide its shape. The two large horns on the head make the animal look especially scary. Predators think twice before trying to make a meal of the thorny devil.

GLOSSARY

BURROW – A tunnel or hole in the ground made or used as a home for an animal.

ENVIRONMENT – Everything around a living animal, which includes land, water, and air.

NOCTURNAL – To be active mainly at night.

PREDATOR – An animal that hunts other animals for food.

PREY – An animal that other animals hunt for food.

PROBOSCIS – The large, fleshy snout, or nose, of an animal.

SNOUT – The long front part of an animal's head that includes the nose.